Dream big, little one! Inside this coloring book, you'll discover a world of possibilities. Each page is filled with motivational tag lines and information about different professions. Explore the exciting world of astronauts, doctors, teachers, scientists, and many more. Learn what these professions are all about and how you can become one too. Let your imagination soar and embrace the power of dreams. You are a dreamer, and your dreams can take you anywhere!

Thank You For Choosing This Book

Thank you for joining us on this exciting journey of dreams and possibilities. We hope this book has sparked your imagination and filled your young mind with inspiration. Remember, you have the power to make your dreams come true. Dream big and reach for the stars!

We request you to leave a rating and provide feedback on Amazon, because your thoughts matter to us.

CONNECT with us on social media, OUR INSTA HANDLE IS . @KIDOPUBLISHING

@KIDOPUBLISHING

WHO IS AN ASTRONAUT?

Astronauts are extraordinary individuals who embark on incredible journeys beyond Earth's atmosphere. They strap themselves into powerful rockets and blast off into space, leaving our planet behind. Once in space, they float weightlessly, observing the wonders of the universe and conducting important scientific experiments.

HOW DO I BECOME ONE?

To become an astronaut, you need to study math, science, and engineering. Stay curious, keep learning, and never stop reaching for the stars!

WHO IS A DOCTOR?

Doctors are everyday heroes who dedicate their lives to helping others stay healthy and happy. They use their knowledge, skills, and compassion to diagnose and treat illnesses, mend broken bones, and even perform life-saving surgeries.

HOW DO I BECOME ONE?

To become a doctor, you'll need to work hard in school and study subjects like biology and chemistry. But it's not just about the books! You'll also need to develop great communication skills and a caring heart.

WHO IS A TEACHER?

Teachers are magical guides who help students unlock their full potential and discover the joy of learning. They create engaging lessons, inspire curiosity, and provide a safe and nurturing environment for their students to grow.

HOW DO I BECOME ONE?

To become a teacher, you'll need a love for knowledge and a passion for shaping young minds. You'll learn how to create lesson plans, lead classroom activities, and be a mentor and role model.

WHO IS AN ENGINEER?

Engineers are problem solvers and innovators who build and create amazing things. They use their knowledge of math and science to design and construct bridges, buildings, robots, and much more.

HOW DO I BECOME ONE?

To become an engineer, you'll need to study hard and have a curious mind. You'll learn about different branches of engineering, such as civil, mechanical, or electrical engineering, and gain hands-on experience with designing and building projects. Find solutions to complex challenges and make the world a better place.

WHO IS A CHEF?

Chefs are culinary experts who master the art of creating delectable dishes. They have a deep passion for food and enjoy exploring flavors and ingredients.

HOW DO I BECOME ONE?

To become a chef, you can start by developing your cooking skills at home and experimenting with various recipes. As you progress, you may consider attending culinary school to learn advanced techniques and gain professional knowledge.

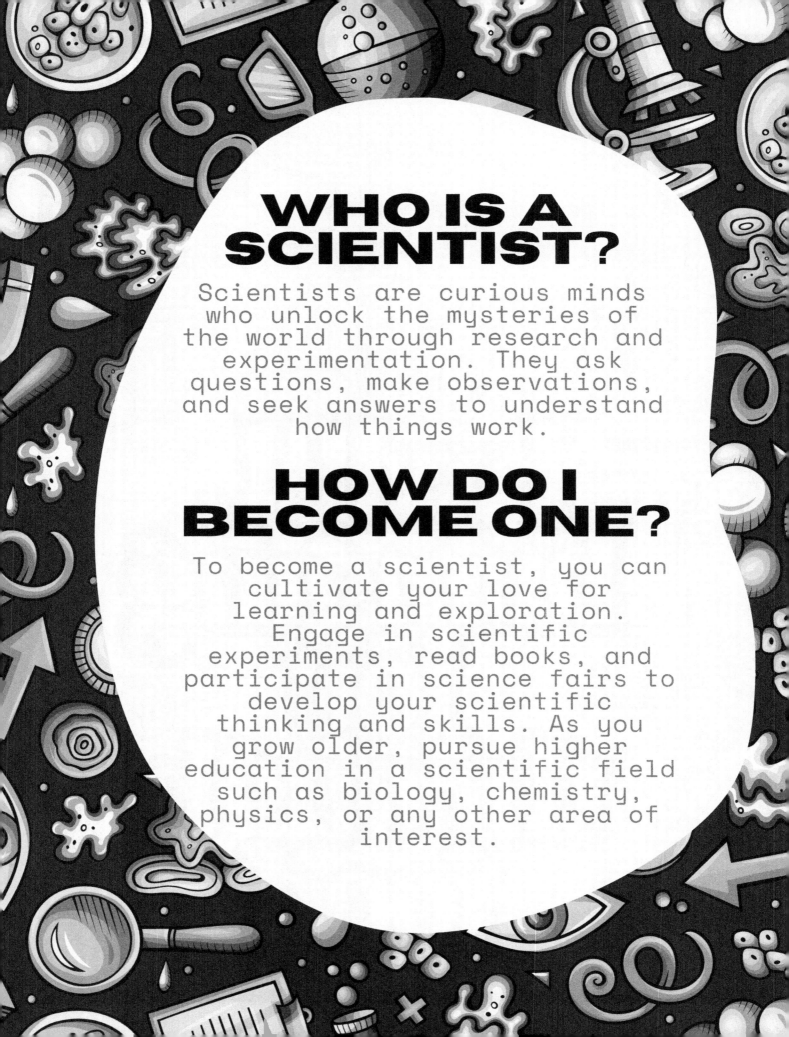

WHO IS A SCIENTIST?

Scientists are curious minds who unlock the mysteries of the world through research and experimentation. They ask questions, make observations, and seek answers to understand how things work.

HOW DO I BECOME ONE?

To become a scientist, you can cultivate your love for learning and exploration. Engage in scientific experiments, read books, and participate in science fairs to develop your scientific thinking and skills. As you grow older, pursue higher education in a scientific field such as biology, chemistry, physics, or any other area of interest.

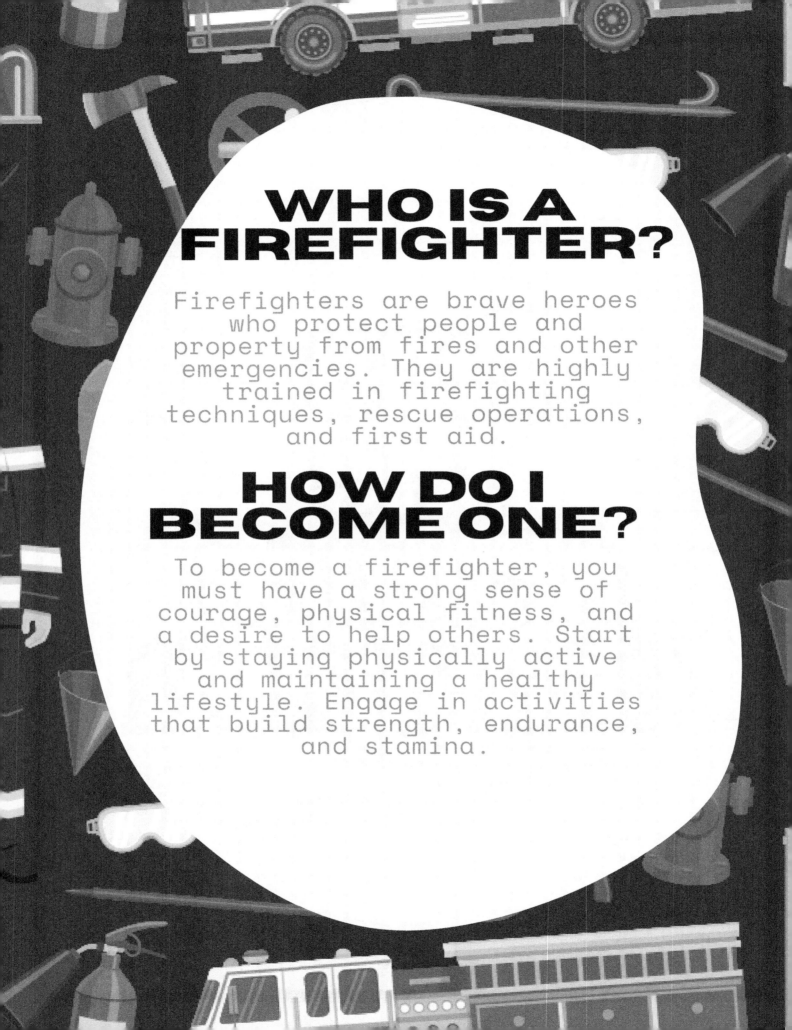

WHO IS A FIREFIGHTER?

Firefighters are brave heroes who protect people and property from fires and other emergencies. They are highly trained in firefighting techniques, rescue operations, and first aid.

HOW DO I BECOME ONE?

To become a firefighter, you must have a strong sense of courage, physical fitness, and a desire to help others. Start by staying physically active and maintaining a healthy lifestyle. Engage in activities that build strength, endurance, and stamina.

WHO IS A POLICE OFFICER?

Police officers are dedicated individuals who work to maintain law and order, ensuring the safety and security of communities.

HOW DO I BECOME ONE?

To become a police officer, you must have a strong sense of justice, integrity, and physical fitness. Start by focusing on your education and maintaining good grades. When you grow up engage in volunteer work with law enforcement agencies to gain practical experience.

WHO IS AN ARTIST?

Artists are creative individuals who express themselves through various forms of art, such as painting, drawing, sculpting, or performing.

HOW DO I BECOME ONE?

To become an artist, embrace your creativity and passion for art from a young age. Explore different art mediums and techniques to find your preferred artistic style. Practice regularly and experiment with different subjects and styles to develop your skills. Take art classes or workshops to learn new techniques and gain insights from experienced artists.

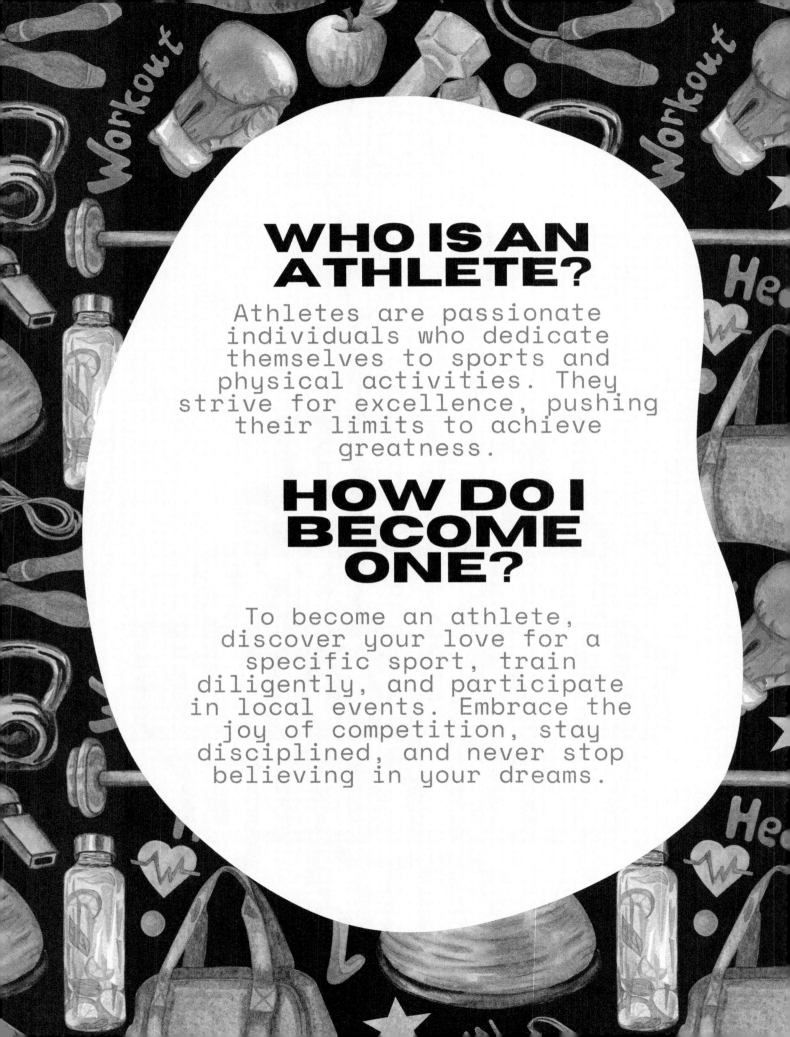

WHO IS AN ATHLETE?

Athletes are passionate individuals who dedicate themselves to sports and physical activities. They strive for excellence, pushing their limits to achieve greatness.

HOW DO I BECOME ONE?

To become an athlete, discover your love for a specific sport, train diligently, and participate in local events. Embrace the joy of competition, stay disciplined, and never stop believing in your dreams.

WHO IS A MUSICIANS?

A musician is a magical creator of melodies and rhythms. They play instruments or sing, filling the world with beautiful sounds that touch our hearts and make us dance with joy.

HOW DO I BECOME ONE?

To become a musician, choose an instrument or use your voice to express your musical talent. Practice regularly, learn from experienced musicians, and explore different music styles. Perform in front of others, join a band or choir, and share your passion with the world. Embrace your creativity, stay dedicated.

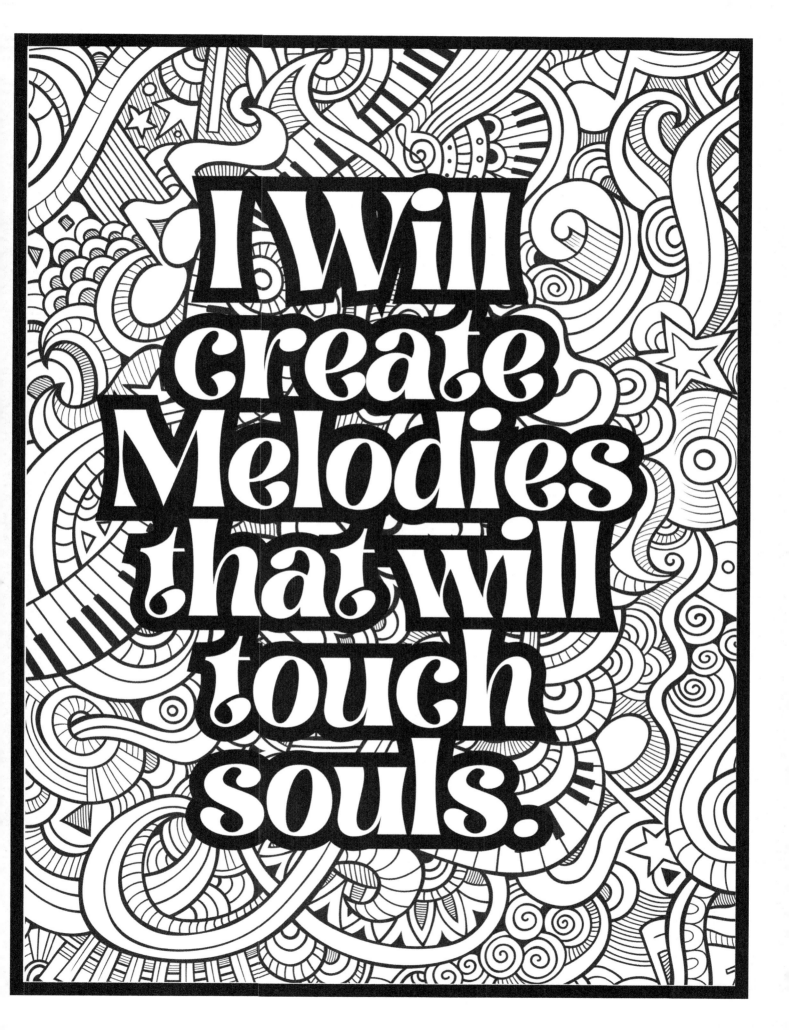

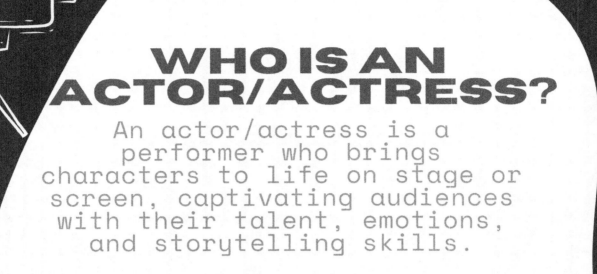

WHO IS AN ACTOR/ACTRESS?

An actor/actress is a performer who brings characters to life on stage or screen, captivating audiences with their talent, emotions, and storytelling skills.

HOW DO I BECOME ONE?

To become an actor/actress, explore your love for acting by participating in school plays, joining drama clubs, and taking acting classes.
Practice expressing emotions, memorizing lines, and developing your unique characters.
Remember to have fun, be confident, and believe in your abilities.

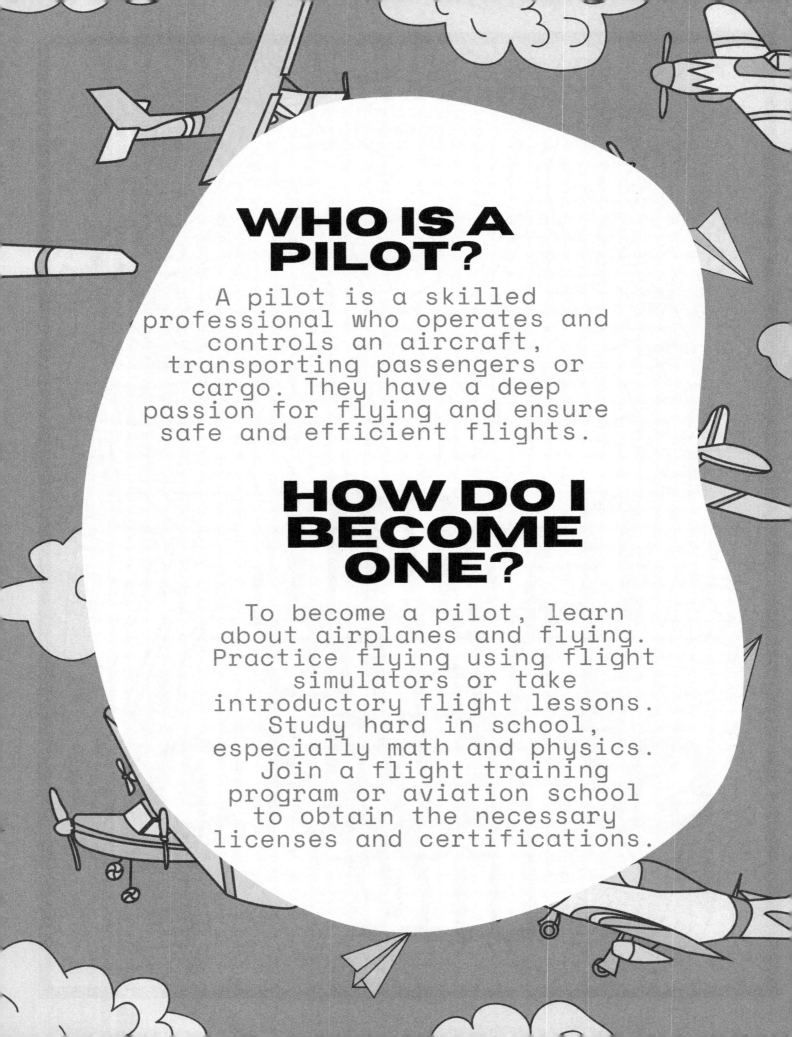

WHO IS A PILOT?

A pilot is a skilled professional who operates and controls an aircraft, transporting passengers or cargo. They have a deep passion for flying and ensure safe and efficient flights.

HOW DO I BECOME ONE?

To become a pilot, learn about airplanes and flying. Practice flying using flight simulators or take introductory flight lessons. Study hard in school, especially math and physics. Join a flight training program or aviation school to obtain the necessary licenses and certifications.

WHO IS AN ARCHITECT?

An architect is a visionary creator of stunning structures. They design spaces that merge functionality and beauty, shaping the world we inhabit with their expertise and imagination.

HOW DO I BECOME ONE?

To become an architect, cultivate your passion for design and construction. Hone your drawing and problem-solving skills. Pursue an architecture degree. Gain practical experience through internships. Learn architectural software and stay updated.

WHO IS FASHION DESIGNER?

A fashion designer is a trendsetter, creating stylish garments that make people feel fabulous. They have an eye for fabric, color, and form, bringing artistry and self-expression to fashion.

HOW DO I BECOME ONE?

To become Fashion Designer, develop a strong sense of style, and learn about textiles and sewing. Attend fashion school or take relevant courses. Build a portfolio of creative designs. Embrace your individuality and inspire with your fashion creations.

WHO IS A VETERINARIAN?

A veterinarian cares for animals, treating their illnesses and ensuring their well-being. They perform surgeries and provide preventive care, dedicating themselves to animal health.

HOW DO I BECOME ONE?

To become a vet, study science and biology in school. Gain animal experience through volunteering or shadowing. Attend vet school, complete internships, and get licensed. Show compassion and dedication to animal welfare.

WHO IS A WRITER?

A writer is a storyteller who weaves words into captivating tales. They create worlds and characters, igniting imagination and evoking emotions through their writing.

HOW DO I BECOME ONE?

To become a writer, read voraciously and write daily. Explore various genres and writing styles. Develop your unique voice and hone your writing skills. Seek feedback and learn from other writers. Embrace creativity, persevere through challenges, and let your words paint the canvas of imagination.

WHO IS A DANCER?

A dancer is a graceful performer who expresses emotions and tells stories through movement. They captivate audiences with their fluidity, precision, and passion.

HOW DO I BECOME ONE?

To become a dancer, start with a dance style that inspires you. Take lessons, practice daily, and learn from experienced dancers. Explore different choreographies and embrace your unique style. Perform on stage, join dance groups, and share your love for dance with the world.

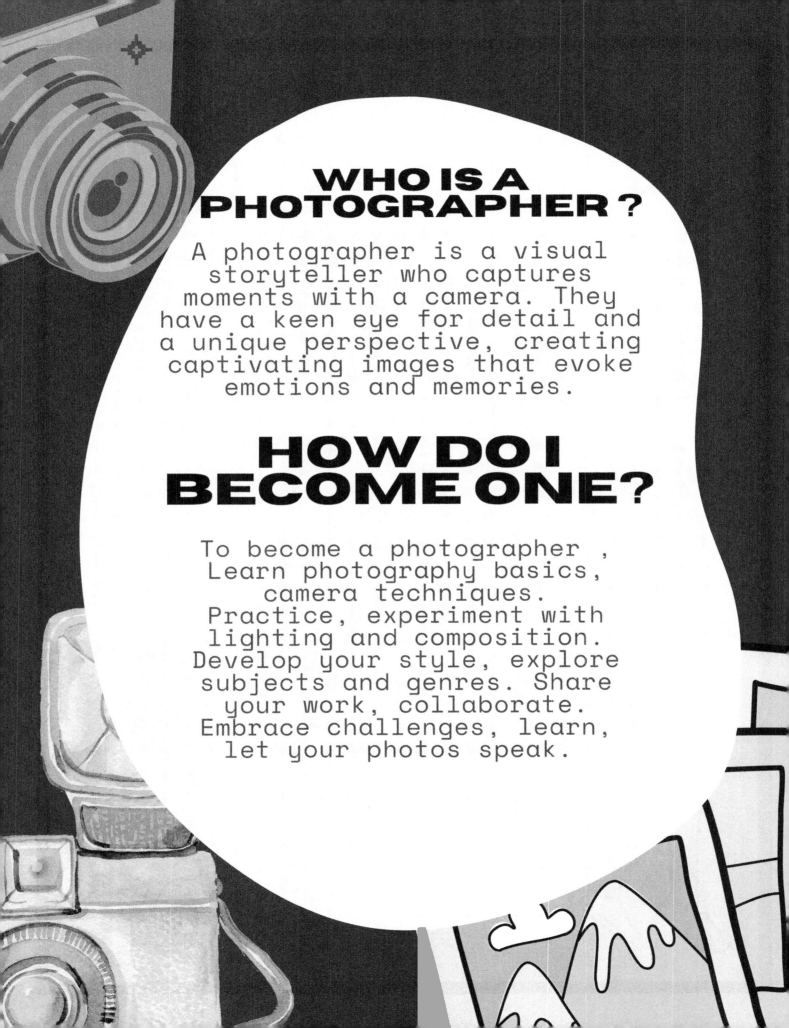

WHO IS A PHOTOGRAPHER ?

A photographer is a visual storyteller who captures moments with a camera. They have a keen eye for detail and a unique perspective, creating captivating images that evoke emotions and memories.

HOW DO I BECOME ONE?

To become a photographer , Learn photography basics, camera techniques. Practice, experiment with lighting and composition. Develop your style, explore subjects and genres. Share your work, collaborate. Embrace challenges, learn, let your photos speak.

WHO IS A LAWYER?

A lawyer is a legal professional who advocates for justice and helps people navigate the complexities of the law. They provide advice, represent clients, and work towards fair outcomes.

HOW DO I BECOME ONE?

To become a Lawyer , Study diligently, earn a law degree. Gain practical experience, internships. Develop strong research and communication skills. Pass the bar exam, obtain a license. Specialize in a specific area of law. Advocate for fairness, uphold justice.

WHO IS A NURSE?

A nurse provides essential medical care and support with compassion. They work in healthcare settings, promoting healing and comfort.

HOW DO I BECOME ONE?

To become a Nurse , Complete nursing education, obtain a license, and gain practical experience. Specialize in a specific area of nursing. Update knowledge and show empathy towards patients.

WHO IS AN ARCHAEOLOGIST?

An archaeologist is a treasure hunter of the past, unearthing ancient artifacts and exploring ancient civilizations. They study clues from artifacts to understand history.

HOW DO I BECOME ONE?

To become an archaeologist, start by exploring history and visiting museums. Learn about ancient artifacts and the tools archaeologists use. Join archaeological camps or clubs to experience excavation firsthand.

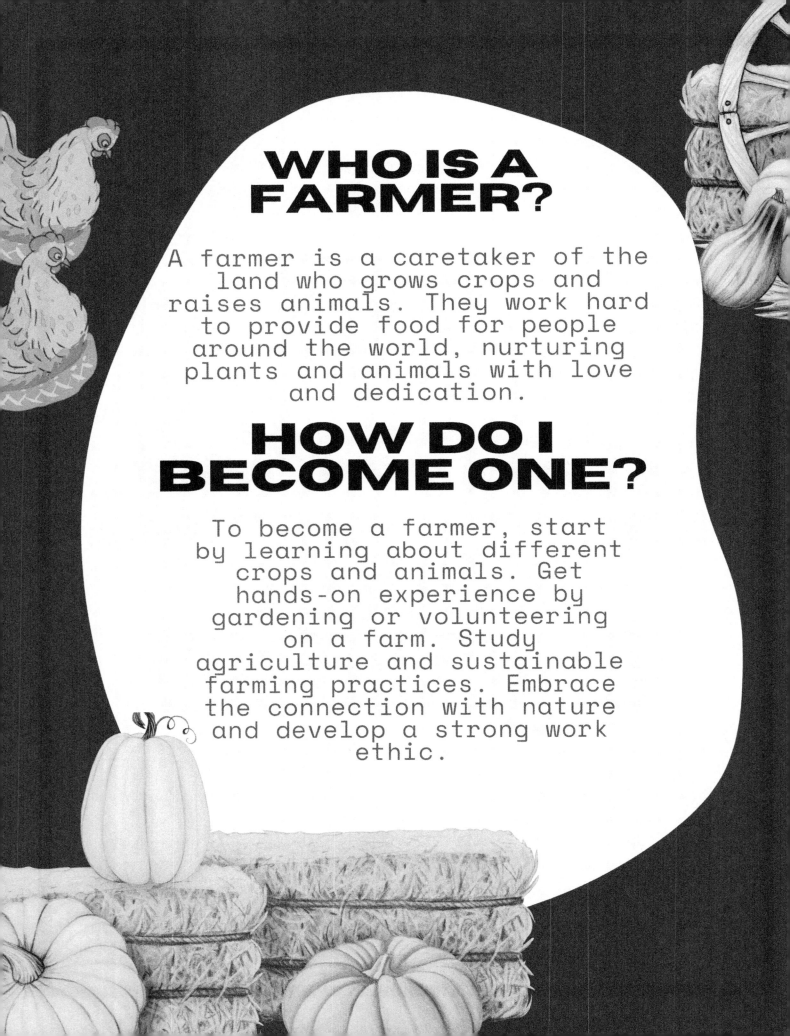

WHO IS A FARMER?

A farmer is a caretaker of the land who grows crops and raises animals. They work hard to provide food for people around the world, nurturing plants and animals with love and dedication.

HOW DO I BECOME ONE?

To become a farmer, start by learning about different crops and animals. Get hands-on experience by gardening or volunteering on a farm. Study agriculture and sustainable farming practices. Embrace the connection with nature and develop a strong work ethic.

WHO IS A JOURNALIST?

A journalist is a curious explorer of stories and events. They gather information and share news with the public through writing or reporting. Journalists keep society informed and hold those in power accountable.

HOW DO I BECOME ONE?

To become a journalist, have a passion for current events and storytelling. Develop strong writing and communication skills. Hone research abilities and fact-check information. Join school newspapers or pursue journalism courses. Embrace curiosity, integrity, and the drive to seek the truth.

BRE

WHO IS A COMPUTER PROGRAMMER?

A computer programmer is a wizard of coding and problem-solving. They write instructions in special languages that computers understand and use their creativity to build software, apps, and websites.

HOW DO I BECOME ONE?

To become a programmer, learn coding basics and explore languages like Python or Java. Solve coding puzzles and join coding communities. Take online courses and get a computer science degree. Build projects and collaborate with others. Keep learning and discover the magic of programming!

WHO IS A MAGICIAN?

A magician is a master of illusions and magic tricks. With their skillful hands and clever tricks, they can make objects disappear, pull rabbits out of hats, and perform mind-boggling feats that amaze and entertain public.

HOW DO I BECOME ONE?

To become a magician, start by learning simple magic tricks and practice them until you can perform them flawlessly. Study the art of misdirection and sleight of hand. Develop your showmanship skills and create your own unique style. Perform in front of friends and family to gain confidence.

WHO IS AN ENTREPRENEUR?

An entrepreneur is a visionary who starts their own business. They identify opportunities, innovate, and create successful ventures. Entrepreneurs are passionate, creative risk-takers who drive economic growth.

HOW DO I BECOME ONE?

To become an entrepreneur, think about what you love to do and how it can help others. Come up with a cool business idea that solves a problem. Make a plan and gather some money to start your business. Stay positive, work hard, and never give up on your dreams. Learn from your mistakes and always keep learning.

WHO IS A SHIP CAPTAIN?

A ship captain commands a vessel, ensuring safe navigation and overseeing operations. They possess extensive maritime knowledge and decision-making skills.

HOW DO I BECOME ONE?

To become a ship captain, gain industry experience, acquire necessary certifications, and develop navigation and leadership skills. Build practical experience and stay updated with industry advancements. With dedication, you can aspire to become a respected ship captain.

WHO IS A DENTIST?

A dentist is a dental care expert who helps keep our teeth healthy and bright. They examine teeth, diagnose dental issues, and provide treatments to prevent and treat oral problems.

HOW DO I BECOME ONE?

To become a dentist, complete a dental degree program, acquire clinical experience, and obtain a dental license. Continuously update your knowledge and skills through continuing education. With compassion and precision, you can become a trusted dentist who brings smiles to people's faces.

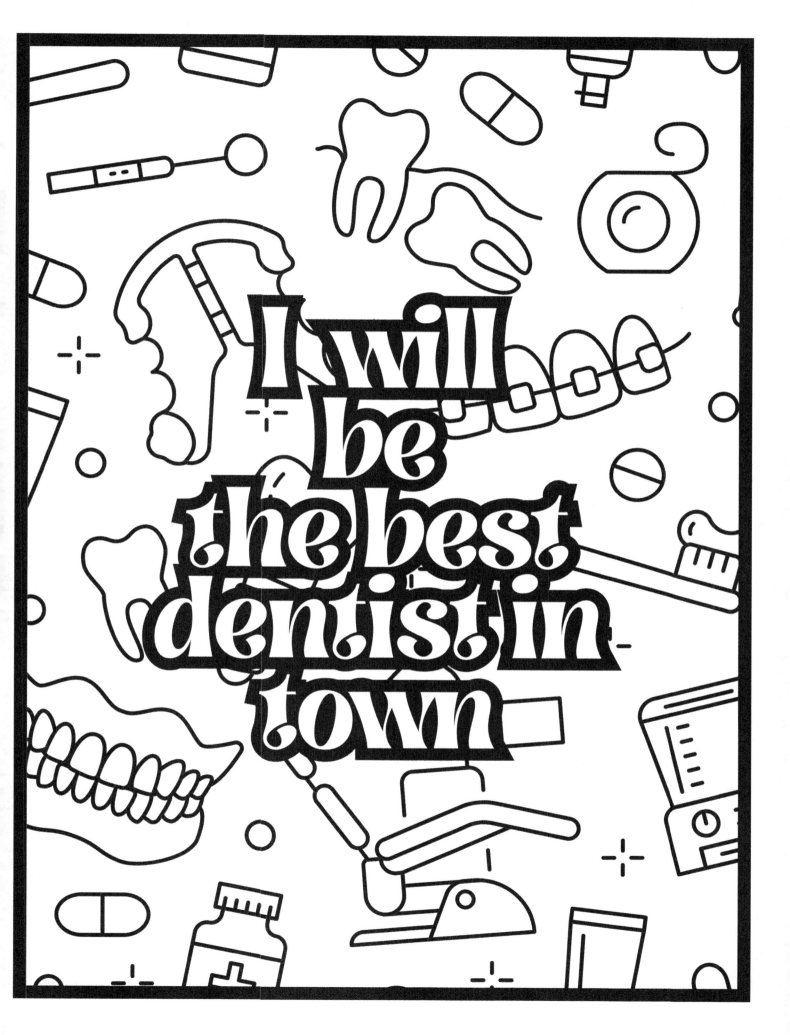

WHO IS A FORMULA 1 RACER

An F1 racer is an elite and fearless driver who competes in Formula 1 races, showcasing exceptional speed, precision, and control.

HOW DO I BECOME ONE?

To become an F1 racer, start with karting and gain experience in various racing categories. Train intensively, honing your driving skills and physical fitness. Seek sponsorship and join professional racing teams. Progress through the ranks, demonstrating exceptional talent and determination. Embrace the thrill of high-speed racing and dream big of becoming an F1 champion.

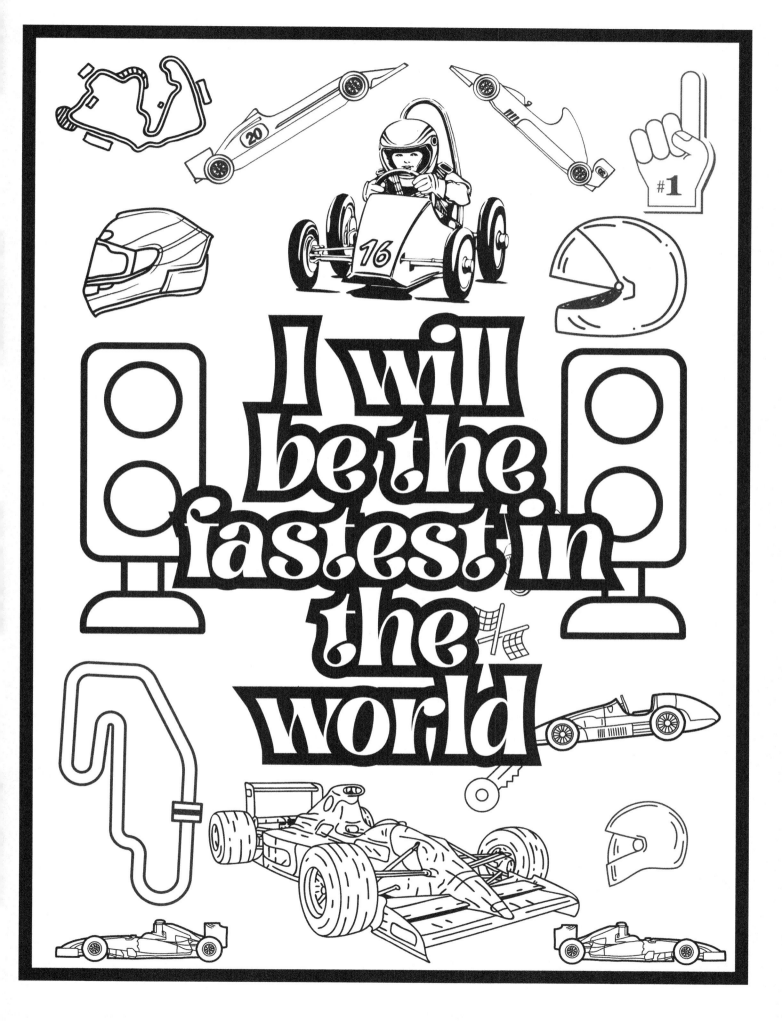

WHO IS A SOLDIER?

A soldier is a brave and dedicated defender who serves in the military to protect their country and its people. They uphold values of honor, courage, and sacrifice.

HOW DO I BECOME ONE?

To become a soldier, develop physical strength and endurance through regular exercise and training. Seek education and training opportunities in military academies or enlist in the armed forces. Learn essential skills, including teamwork, discipline, and tactical knowledge. Embrace a sense of duty and patriotism, ready to serve your nation with integrity and resilience.

WHO IS AN INFLUENCER?

An influencer inspires others through creativity, using their platform to make a positive impact.

HOW DO I BECOME ONE?

To become a Influencer discover your unique talents and interests, create compelling content that resonates with your audience, engage with your followers, collaborate with brands, and spread positivity through your online presence.

WHO IS A JUDGE?

A judge is a wise and fair decision-maker in the courtroom. They listen carefully, analyze evidence, and uphold justice with integrity and impartiality.

HOW DO I BECOME ONE?

To become a Judge Study hard, excel in academics, and pursue a law degree. Gain experience as a lawyer, develop strong analytical and communication skills, and demonstrate a deep understanding of the law. Uphold ethics, seek opportunities in the judiciary, and strive for excellence to make a difference in the legal system.

Party God's Alibi

IT WAS A PARTY

EVERYONE PARTIED QUITE HEARTY

WE RAN OUT OF DRINKS

HAH HAH NO WE DIDN'T, I'M PARTY GOD

PARTY FOREVER

PARTY FOREVER

PARTY FOREVER

Yes thank you this was very helpful

I'd helped PB set up the hall earlier that day, so I thought I'd drop in and see how things were going.

I'm listening...

When I got there, I saw Finn and Jake with some skeletons outside.

Wait, wait: this is the first thing that corroborates anything! Finn and Jake mentioned that too!

Oh. Cool.

Anyway it turns out they were all protesting. They wanted the princesses to sign a joint statement reclassifying grave-yards as "skeleton farms"?

No, wait. "RAD skeleton farms."

I'm sorry, but nobody gets seconds until everyone's had firsts.

But I'm hungry! Food goes right through me!!

I'D DEMONSTRATE IF YOU LET ME.

STICKS & STONES MAY BREAK MY BONES BUT PREJUDICIAL GRAVEYARD CLASSIFICATION REALLY HURTS ME!

PRI BU DU

NO BON ABOUT EQUALI

ANTI-SKELE BIAS CHILLS M TO THE ONE

DID YOU MOVE TODAY THANK YOUR SKELETON!

OH MY GLOB, WERE ANY OF YOU GUYS EVEN AT THE SAME PLACE?

REMIND ME TO NEVER ASK ANY OF YOU TO REMEMBER ANYTHING EVER

22

Ice King, I hover before you a broken princess. You're my last hope, and if you can't tell me something that makes sense, then I think my star actually IS lost...FOREVER!!

Ha ha, WOW, have you come to the wrong place! These stanky old wizard eyes aren't good for that sort of thing at all!

mek

"Listen: I'd heard about Bubblegum's party and I figured I should crash it. It sounded like a cool place to meet babes, you know?"

Hey, anyone here want to meet a lonely man??

"But I got kicked out in like five seconds."

Oh my glob get OUT of here, Ice King! This is a babes-only zone!!

But I'M a #1 babe!

You believe me when I say that, right?

Aha! So you were SO UPSET from my AWESOME RULES ENFORCEMENT that you came back that very night to steal from me??

mek

What? No! No, I went home and wrote in my diary until it was time for bed!

You want to read it? It mentions your star! I'll prove it!

DATING ON THIN ICE

THE SEMI-FICTIONALIZED DIARY OF ONE MAN WHOSE EMOTIONS WERE ALL TOO REAL

"As LSP kicked me out, the star on her head seemed to symbolize how, much like the actual stars themselves, like the ones in space I mean, these smokin' hot megababes were destined to remain forever beyond my reach.

PASS

Hey, are you sure your star didn't just, you know...**FALL OUT** somewhere?

Well it never fell out before, Ice King!

I don't know. I thought it had to be one of you guys since you were the only ones who left before I noticed my star was missing, but now...I don't know **ANYTHING** anymore. I guess...I guess it's really gone, huh?

And now I'll never see it again and have to wear this stupid patch forever and it's not even that hot.

LSP, I know a thing or two about loss, and you know what I've learned?

Sometimes all you can do is tell yourself that losing it was the best thing that could've happened to you, over and over and **OVER** again until you finally, **FINALLY**, believe it.

UM HELLO ICE KING THAT'S THE WORST ADVICE EVER!!

mek

I'm **OUT OF HERE**, loser criminal best friends!!

I'ma find my star on my own, and I don't need **ANY** of you jerks!!

Hey, LSP. Wake up!

Huh?

We couldn't find your old star either, so we made you a new one!

We all pitched in with different substances!

Do you like it?

AHHHHH! I LOVE IT I LOVE IT I LOVE IT!!

And you all made it for me together?!

Yep!

AHHH, IT'S TOO PERFECT!! THIS MEANS THERE'S GONNA BE A PART OF Y'ALL THAT'S INSIDE ME FOREVER!!

You guys are the best ever and EVERYTHING RULES AND I LOVE EVERYONE!!

YOU KNOW, NORMALLY IN THESE HAPPY ENDING SITUATIONS I SUGGEST A LITTLE SOMETHING THAT STARTS WITH "PAR"

AND ENDS WITH "TY"

AND IS THE WORD "PARTY" WHEN YOU BRING THE TWO HALVES TOGETHER

Oh my glob, Party God...

...I THOUGHT YOU'D NEVER ASK.

PUZZLE TIME

FINN AND JAKE'S TOTES EPIC PUZZLE THINGS!

For Finn and Jake, cracking radical mysteries, solving puzzles and unravelling cryptic conundrums is good training for questing. So get on your questing gear and get ready for some training of your own.

WORDSEARCH

Hidden in this grid are eight characters from the Land of Ooo! When you've found them all, rearrange the highlighted letters to discover a lumping adorable character!

CINNAMON BUN
GORK
CAKE
GELATIN MAN

THE LICH
ICECLOPS
TONYA
KIM

J	U	S	B	R	E	L	E	A	A	I	K	O
I	N	I	E	U	H	H	K	Y	C	R	A	M
K	F	U	T	B	U	H	A	E	O	R	V	M
D	I	O	B	V	G	I	C	M	S	F	M	N
X	V	K	Y	N	V	L	N	I	B	J	C	A
R	G	R	M	H	O	A	K	U	L	O	C	M
F	W	O	J	P	Z	M	T	A	E	E	U	N
B	J	G	S	B	T	O	A	K	C	S	H	I
P	C	R	O	W	N	O	I	N	W	M	A	T
S	N	I	R	Y	T	I	Z	A	N	U	K	A
H	J	K	A	T	G	F	R	Q	M	I	W	L
Y	W	O	I	M	I	Y	X	Y	M	D	C	E
Z	I	V	G	U	N	T	E	R	T	H	S	G

NUMBER PYRAMID

The Ice King has trapped Princess Bubblegum in his mountain, and won't let her leave until she's heard all his fan fiction! Fill in the squares so that each pair matches the number above, and help Finn and Jake get to the top and save her!

20		
	11	
4		

TRIVIA OF RIGHTEOUSNESS PART 1

1. Where does Finn find the Enchiridion?
2. TRUE OR FALSE: Finn sings a song called "All Messed Up Inside"
3. TRUE OR FALSE: Jake loves to eat, but he can't cook
4. Jake's most delicious sandwich contains:
   a. Tears
   b. Pastrami
   c. The soul of a salmon

BMO IMPOSTER

Dude! Finn and Jake's loyal friend has been lost among a bunch of duplicates! Help them by identifying the true BMO, and restore order to Ooo!

SIGN ZOMBIE SCRAMBLE

Finn and Jake are lost in the Evil Forest, and the Sign Zombies are after them! Follow the maze to guide the heroes to safety, but beware of traps and monsters.

START

FINISH

THE MAGICAL LAND OF Ooo.
FINN & JAKE'S SWEET TREEHOUSE.

Cock a doodle doo.

Thanks, Allen.

A doo.

Get up Jake. Make-a-me breakfast time.

Don't **WANNA** breakfast. Wanna snooze.

Okay! I'll make breakfast.

HA! You can't make no breakfast.

Just because you always do it doesn't mean I can't!

Halt! Who goes there!

Me. Finn. I need eggs and milk and France and butter. I'm making french toast.

No! You can't cook! You'll **RUIN IT.**

What?

You made a SANDWICH.

You made FOOD.

JAKE, YOU KNOW HOW TO MAKE FOOD!

Well, like I still can't make breakfast or whatever.

Am I gonna have to make sandwiches for all those armies out there?

No, Jake. We're going to need MUCH more from you than that.

CONTINUED AFTER PUZZLE PAGE.

SNEAK PEAK AT SOME OF THE UPCOMING ACTION!

You know, I LIKE this cave!

Well yeah, man

WILL A JOURNEY TO THE CENTER OF JAKE REVEAL HIS SANDWICH MAKING MAGIC? SEE YOU THERE!

The cave is YOU.

Man, I want a sandwich.

Oh REALLY? Gosh, I'm sure NOBODY else feels that way. You know, among EVERYONE who's here to raid the kingdom and take all the food, including sandwiches.

I want TACOS!

PUZZLE TIME

MARCELINE'S DAREDEVIL GAMES!

Staying smart is as important as being fearless, especially when there are pranks to devise! Help the Vampire Queen keep her wits sharp with these algebraic puzzles!

CHUD CHASE

Finn and Jake have wandered into a cave in the Desert of Doom, and it's full of Chuds! Follow the maze to guide the heroes out of the cave, but beware of the humanoid monsters!

ANAGRAM SLAM

Can you solve these anagrams to reveal the awesome characters?

MEAN RELIC

SMALL HEALER

PECAN DEPLOY

TUSK RENTER

CRUMBLING LEAP

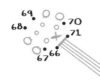

VAMPIRE FADE

Marceline has hit an awesome new bass note so powerful it has nearly obliterated her! Bring her back to reality by drawing in the details.

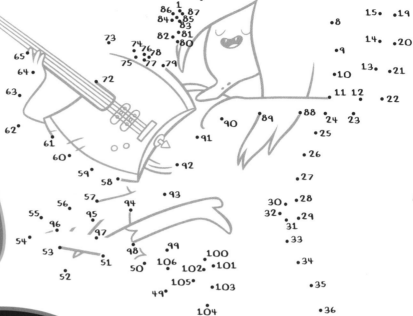

LAND OF OOO SUDOKU

Marceline's taking a break from her ax bass to make sure she's as smart as P-Bubs! Help her out by placing Chocoberry, Snail, Tiny Goblin and Ms Pig so that they appear once in each row and column.

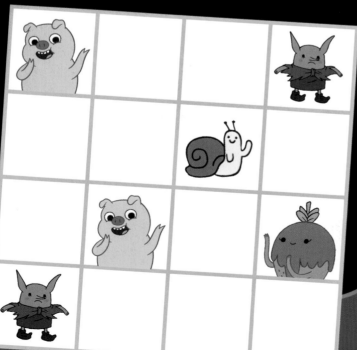

TRIVIA OF RIGHTEOUSNESS PART 2

1. **TRUE OR FALSE:** Princess Bubblegum's real name is Bonnibel

2. **TRUE OR FALSE:** Tree Trunks is a pygmy hippo

3. **TRUE OR FALSE:** Marceline can play the banjo ukulele

4. Where does Jake discover the businessmen in "Business Time"?
   a. Lost in the Spooky Forest
   b. Stuck in an iceberg in Iceberg Lake
   c. Floating on a raft on Lake Butterscotch

Chill out, man!

It's just my stomach!

Your STOMACH would have thought I was food! It would have taken ALL MY NUTRIENTS.

I like having those nutrients around, man.

No way. I'd be all "Hey body! Don't digest Finn. He's cool!"

Found him! Looks like you zapped Finn into my tummy zone.

Ah! I specifically wanted to avoid hazards like your digestive tract!

Sorry, Finn! I tried to complete the miniaturization teleport near the source of Jake's sandwich magic and uh...

I guess if it was just going to send you to his stomach we could have just shrunk you out here and had Jake eat you.

Ha ha! Frontier science!

Ha.

"I'm Princess Bubblegum and I got excited about EXPERIMENTS and didn't think this through! Sorry!"

That's basically what she's saying.

Ha ha! Sounds right!

Jake, We've identified the tiny spark of food creation ability that you've magically retained...

HERE. Near Finn.

Under normal circumstances, when all of Ooo isn't CURSED to forget how to make food...

We would ALL be COMPLETELY glowing under this light frequency. Not just this little bit inside you.

If Finn can retrieve whatever that is that's allowed you to retain your ability to make sandwiches...

BWIP

Then we might be able to grow it, cure everyone, and GET THEM TO NOT RAID THE KINGDOM for our LEFTOVERS.

WE'RE GETTING PRETTY HANGRY, PRINCESS!

WHY WOULD YOU THINK I'VE FORGOTTEN THAT?!

Don't worry, Princess! Me and Finn are ON THE MOVE.

Now, I must FOCUS on my avatar with Finn. Excuse me.

POP

Never been in THIS part of my body before.

What do you mean THIS part?

Eh, haven't been in MOST of it really.

Uh oh.

Invader!

That looks like immune system stuff.

Destroy invader! Protect the host!

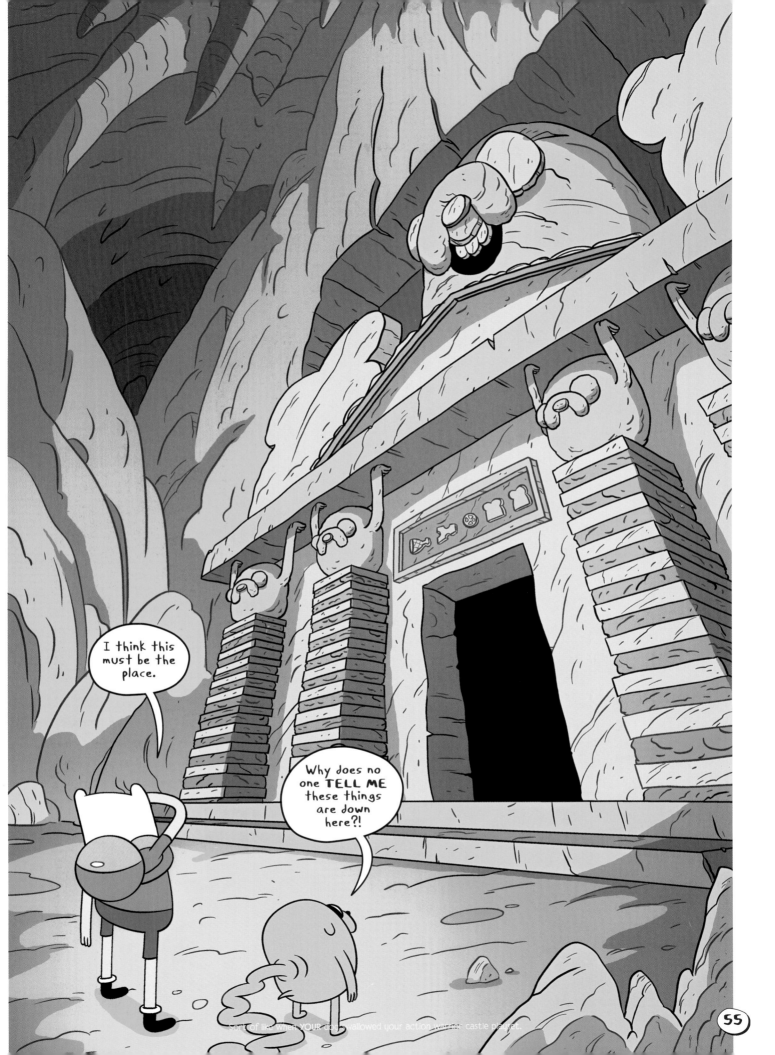

Uh, hey there guy.

Who are YOU?

What? I'm JAKE. You know who I am!

I don't.

I'm like... ALL AROUND YOU, MAN! I'm your king or something!

Look! I can change stuff with MY WILL.

hhhhhh

ARRRGHHHHH

POP

Ah!

It IS you! The EATER.

YEAH, that's right, baby--wait the what now?

Ah, welcome! The eater! The one who sent us... THE CRYSTAL OF PERFECT SANDWICH!

THAT WHICH CREATED US!

I think that's what we were looking for, buddy!

A perfectly preserved... tiny piece...

Of the greatest sandwich I EVER HAD. I remember that sandwich!

It must have gotten stuck like that! And gave me POWERS.

Looks like it made part of you into a PRETTY CUTE princess too, buddy.

Hee hee hee

What?! Oh jeeze! YOU TWO WOULD BE PERFECT TOGETHER!

She's a little of ME, your best friend! And she's a little of SANDWICH, the best food!

And she's TOTAL PRINCESS.

You'd have to stay in here. She can't leave.

I'd miss you, but I can come visit! I--

Dude. Chill. I don't want to go out with ANY princesses right now.

My sword lazers only work if I have perfect health!

Don't wanna risk a BROKEN HEART.

Seriously? Maybe we talk about that sword later.

What are you talking about?

Is it sandwiches?

GRAAH!

I'm sorry Jake... LAZER SWORD COME TO ME.

ZAP ZAP ZAP

♪ We have got a problem, girl ♪ You be chasin' me ♪ But I'll stop this squabble, girl ♪ With these lazers, see?

AAAAA MY GUTS!

Now's our chance! Smash stuff until food comes out!

WHAT?! There's no—

THERE'S NO FOOD IN ANY OF THIS!

Feel the burps. Believe in the burps.

YUSS!

BUUURRRRRPPP

Princess! I'm out! Size me back up!

I think I heard a tiny Finn!

Seems likely, given the circumstances!

GASP!

That... gem...

If... that piece... combines with that piece...

And then it has... that condiment...

That texture... juxtaposed with **THAT** texture.

Then... that could work... WITH ANYTHING!

I REMEMBER HOW TO MAKE FOOD!

I have to **SHOW EVERYONE.**

You used your sword lazers inside my guts! You **REALLY HURT ME.**

What?! Dude, those sandwich people turned into **MONSTERS.** I had to!

Plus it made you burp me out.

CLACK

I **TOLD YOU,** I wouldn't let any of my body hurt you!

You weren't there! You couldn't stop them!

Be honest! You just wanted to use the **SWORD LAZERS** you love so much!

That sword is **CHANGING YOU.**

YOU be honest! Part of you **DEEP DOWN** didn't want to give up your sandwich powers, and it **ATTACKED ME.**

I... remember how to make food!

It all makes sense!

That crystalized hunk of sandwich is giving me some ideas!

Let's celebrate!

A **FEAST!** Let's have A **FEAST!**

NO. You just tried to **RANSACK** my kingdom, and now you expect me to **HOST A PARTY?**

GET LOST. We can all talk on Monday.

PUZZLE TIME

ICE KING'S SUMMER STUMPERS!

Ice King is having some quality time with Gunter and tackling some righteous puzzles! Help them impress any passing Princess by working out the answers to these rhombus riddles!

CIRCLE OF MYSTERY

Some letters from the alphabet are missing from this circle. What character do the letters spell?

___ ___ ___ ___ ___ ___

L G W
Z U K H
E R B V
J A F S
Q C X P
I D

PRINCESS BUBBLEGUM'S PERFECT SANDWICH

Ice King has captured Princess Bubblegum, and he's trying to win her affections by making her a perfect sandwich! Help him impress her by placing each ingredient so that it appears once in each row and column.

TRIVIA OF RIGHTEOUSNESS PART 3

1. What was the name of Ice King when he was still a human man?

2. Who is the keeper of the Enchiridion?

3. In "Simon & Marcy", what do Simon and Marcy go in search of to cure Marcy's illness?

4. How do Finn and Jake finally defeat the Ice King's computer virus in "A Glitch Is a Glitch"?

5. What do you do in a Mallow Tea Ceremony?
   a Drink marshmallow tea in the Tree Fort
   b Brew tea inside a giant marshmallow
   c Drink tea while bouncing on giant marshmallows

LEMONGRAB LIKENESS

Can you help the Ice King spot the five differences between these two pictures?

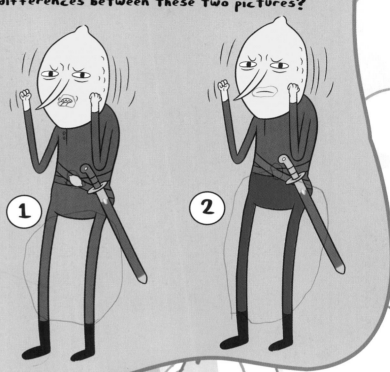

FIX THE GLITCH

Oh Glob, the Ice King has accidentally cast a spell on himself and Gunter and sent them to another dimension. Copy the drawing in the grid to bring them back.

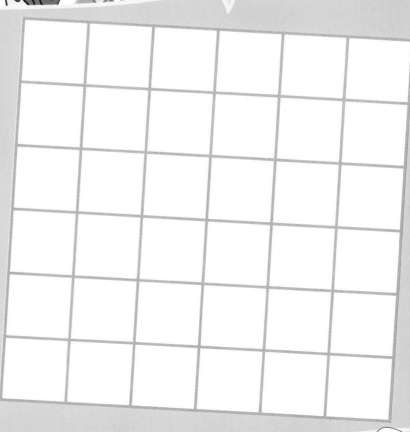

Writers: Chris Roberson & Georgia Roberson (Age 8)   Artist: Lucy Knisley

THE ANSWERS

PAGE 28. FINN AND JAKE'S TOTES EPIC PUZZLE THINGS!

TRIVIA OF RIGHTEOUSNESS
PART 1:
1. At the top of Mount Cragdor
2. FALSE: the song is "All Gummed Up Inside"?
3. FALSE: Jake is a talented chef
4. A Tears

NUMBER PYRAMID:
20
9 11
4 5 6

SIGN ZOMBIE:
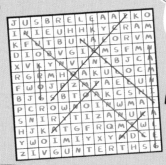

SCRAMBLE:
WORDSEARCH:
ANSWER: CUTE KING

BMO IMPOSTER: 2

PAGE 46. MARCELINE'S DAREDEVIL GAMES

TRIVIA OF RIGHTEOUSNESS
PART 2:
1. TRUE
2. FALSE: she is a pygmy elephant
3. TRUE
4. Answer: B Stuck in an iceberg in Iceberg Lake

ANAGRAM SLAM:
Mean Relic = Marceline
Small Healer = Marshall Lee
Pecan Deploy = Candy People
Tusk Renter = Tree Trunks
Crumbling Leap = Prince Gumball

CHUD CHASE:

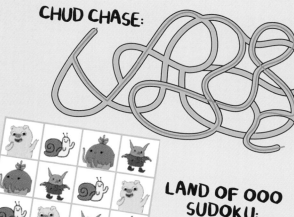

LAND OF OOO SUDOKU:

PAGE 64. ICE KING'S SUMMER STUMPERS

TRIVIA OF RIGHTEOUSNESS PART 3:
1. Simon Petrikov
2. Mannish Man
3. Chicken soup
4. They eat Jake's hair
5. Answer: C Drink tea while bouncing on giant marshmallows.

CIRCLE OF MYSTERY:
M-O-N-T-Y,

PRINCESS BUBBLEGUM'S PERFECT SANDWICH:

LEMONGRAB LIKENESS:
1. Lemon on is belt is missing.
2. His mouth has changed.
3. Trousers have changed colour.
4. Buttons on his top are missing.
5. Handle of his sword has changed colour.

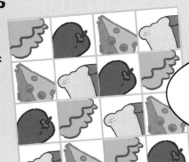

Did you find me? I was on pages 8, 29, 32, 47, 52, 65.